VALENTINE'S DAY

A TRUE BOOK

by
Dana Meachen Rau

Children's Press®
A Division of Scholastic Inc.

New York Toronto London Auckland Sydney
Mexico City New Delhi Hong Kong
Danbury, Connecticut

Children make cards for
Valentine's Day.

Reading Consultant
Nanci Vargus
Primary Multiage Teacher
Decatur Township Schools
Indianapolis, Indiana

Library of Congress Cataloging-in-Publication Data

Rau, Dana Meachen, 1971-
    Valentine's Day / by Dana Meachen Rau.
        p. cm. – (A true book)
    Includes bibliographical references and index.
    ISBN 0-516-22244-9 (lib. bdg.) 0-516-27346-9 (pbk.)
I. Valentine's Day—Juvenile literature. [I. Valentine's Day. 2. Holidays.] I.
Title. II. Series.
GT4925 .R38 2001
394.2618—dc21   00-060250

Contents

On Valentine's Day, people often share their feelings with hugs and kisses.

A Day for Love

Every day people show their love to their families, friends, and even pets through their words or actions. But there is one special day of the year when people all over the world celebrate their love. That day is February 14, Valentine's Day.

The history of Valentine's Day as a day of love began centuries ago in the time of the Roman Empire. In ancient Rome, February 14 was a holiday to honor Juno. Juno was the queen of all the Roman gods and goddesses, and the goddess of women and marriage. The Romans believed that if they prayed to Juno, she would help the young people get married.

During the day, they held exciting activities. They wrote

Juno, the Roman goddess of women and marriage

the names of young girls on slips of paper and placed them into an urn. Each young boy drew (or took) a girl's name from the urn. He would then be paired with that girl for another festival to honor the god Lupercus (LU-per-kus) that started the next day. The hope was that during the next day's festival the boy and girl would fall in love and later get married.

Legends of St. Valentine

At the end of the Roman Empire, Christianity began to spread across Europe. Fewer Roman gods and goddesses were honored with festivals. Even though the Christians still celebrated these festivals, they thought that the Roman names were unholy. So they

9

eventually changed the Roman names to Christian ones.

In A.D. 486, Pope Gelasius (jel-A-shuss), the head of the Christian church, forbid the Roman people to hold the festival that celebrated Lupercus. He didn't think it honored the Christian church. He replaced it with another festival that would allow people to meet, fall in love, and marry. He named it after the Christian saint of love, Saint Valentine, because of all the legends that surrounded his life.

According to historical records, there were three saints named Valentine. But the facts of each are unclear. One legend is that Valentine was an early Christian priest who lived in Rome during the third century. At the time, Emperor Claudius II wanted everyone to pray to the

Roman gods. But Valentine wouldn't because he believed in the Christian church. So Claudius threw him in jail. While in jail, Valentine fell in love with the blind daughter of a guard. On February 14, Claudius ordered the guards to cut off Valentine's head. Before he was taken away, Valentine gave a love note to the blind girl. When she opened it, a miracle occurred. Her sight returned, and she

This young boy reads a love note that was sent to him on Valentine's Day.

could read his love note that he had signed, "From your Valentine."

In another legend, Emperor Claudius II created a law that said no young man could marry. Claudius was having a hard time finding young men for his army. But Valentine didn't think that was right. So he performed marriages between young men and women in secret. When Claudius discovered

An almond tree bloomed near Saint Valentine's grave.

this, he had Valentine killed on February 14. After Valentine was buried, an almond tree near his grave burst with pink flowers as a sign of love, and all the birds chose mates.

Whichever legend seems more believable, both stories tell of the importance of true love.

Finding a Sweetheart

Over time, people started to believe that February 14, St. Valentine's Day, was a day to find one's sweetheart. During the Middle Ages in England, people looked to nature for some help. They believed that February 14 was the day that birds, especially doves, began

People believed that doves selected their mates on St. Valentine's Day.

to choose their mates. So, the people thought that the same day might be the best one for them to fall in love, too.

In the 1500s, people chose valentines by drawing names from a basket (left). In the 1800s, people bought valentines at a store (right).

People had other unique ideas about Valentine's Day. Before bed, a young woman would pin five bay leaves to her pillow or would eat a hard-boiled egg, including the shell. If she dreamed about the man that she loved that night, she would marry him within the year. Others practiced a tradition similar to the ancient Romans' idea of drawing names. A woman wrote men's names on slips of paper and rolled them in balls of clay. She dropped them in a bowl of water. Whichever name came out of the clay first and floated to the top was the name of her future husband. Others believed that the first unmarried man that a woman would see on the morning of Valentine's Day would be the man she would marry.

In France, older people of a town would gather together the young men and women. They would then pair the men and women into couples. The young women would prepare a large dinner. Afterwards, they would all go to an elegant ball. Often, each couple would later marry.

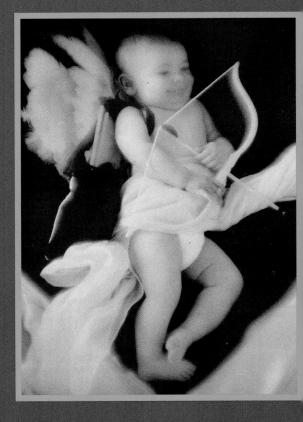

People often decorate for Valentine's Day with special symbols of the holiday.

- Cupid was the son of Venus, who was the Roman goddess of love and beauty. He flew around and shot people with invisible arrows that made them fall instantly in love.

- Doves have been used for centuries as messengers. People used to tie letters to their thin legs and then let them fly away to deliver them. On Valentine's Day, doves are thought of as the messengers of love.

Valentine's Day

- Since ancient times, people have believed that one's heart is where someone feels love for someone else.

- The colors of Valentine's Day are pink, red, and white.

Sending Valentines

February 14 is a day to send valentine cards, or "valentines." Historians believe that a Frenchman named Duke Charles of Orleans was the first person to send valentines. While he was a prisoner in the Tower of London in 1415, the Duke wrote many love letters

Duke Charles of Orleans (left) was held prisoner in the Tower of London (below) in 1415.

and poems to his wife. In them, he often mentioned the name St. Valentine.

In Europe in the 1600s, people began to send each other valentines that they made themselves. They attached ribbons, bows, and lace to decorate them. They looked at books called "Valentine Writers." These were books filled with poetry that the people included in their valentines.

People in earlier times read poems to their loved ones.

To my Valentine

Commercial valentines, such as these, were first produced in the 1800s.

Valentine Greeting

In the United States, people also made handmade valentines. They took their valentines very seriously. If a man sent a woman a valentine, it was almost like he asked for her hand in marriage.

Commercial valentines first appeared in the 1800s. Machines produced the cards so that many could be made at one time. At first, the valentines were very simple. But by the 1840s, they became just as fancy as handmade ones. Some commercial valentines were very expensive. The fanciest valentines were created in England from 1840 to 1860, during the reign of Queen Victoria.

Valentines were often signed and sent by a secret admirers. The receivers had to guess who loved them enough to send them valentines.

Have you ever received
a valentine from a
secret admirer?

America's First Valentine

Esther Howland (1828-1904) was the first person to create valentines to sell in the United States. Her father had a store in Worcester, Massachusetts, where he sold books, paper goods, and European valentines. One day Esther decided that she would create prettier cards than the European ones. She made a few by hand with ribbons and lace and sold them in the store.

Then, Esther's brother took a dozen of her cards on a business trip. When he returned, he had orders worth more than five thousand dollars. So Esther set up an area in her parents' house and started to make the cards. After hiring people to help her, she was

Children often make their
own valentines at school to
give to family and friends.

soon on her way to creating a large business for herself. Orders poured in. She sold cards for five to ten dollars each, which was a lot of money back then. For several years, she was the main, if not the only, American designer and maker of valentines.

Gifts from the Heart

There are many kinds of things you can give or share with someone on Valentine's Day. Here are a few ideas:

• A soft, cuddly teddy bear is a fun way to say Happy Valentine's Day to a friend.

• A basket of freshly baked cookies is a yummy treat. Just be careful not to eat too many at once!

• People give each other flowers as a way to show affection.

• People can buy cards at the store or make them. One way to create a homemade greeting is by using some construction paper, doilies, glue, and glitter.

• A heart-shaped box of chocolates is a special gift for someone you love.

• Sharing some hugs and spending time with loved ones are some of the best ways to celebrate Valentine's Day.

Sharing Love

Today, Valentine's Day is celebrated most in the United States, Canada, Mexico, France, Great Britain, and Australia.

February 14 is one of the busiest holidays for the post office. More than one billion valentines are sent each year.

The post office handles millions of cards each year for Valentine's Day.

Towns with special names, such as Loveland, Colorado, Darling, Pennsylvania, or Love, Mississippi, receive the most mail. Many people send their cards to these towns so that the postmaster can postmark their cards and then resend them with the town's romantic name.

Valentine's Day is a wonderful day to show others how you feel about them.

We can show people how we feel about them by sending cards or giving hugs.

To Find Out More

Here are more places to learn about Valentine's Day and other holidays:

Books

Bulla, Clyde Robert. **The Story of Valentine's Day.** HarperCollins Publishers, 1999.

Corwin, Judith Hoffman. **Valentine Crafts.** Franklin Watts, 1994.

Fradin, Dennis Brindell. **Valentine's Day.** Enslow Publishers, 1990.

Roop, Peter and Connie. **Let's Celebrate Valentine's Day.** The Millbrook Press, 1999.

Ross, Kathy. **Crafts for Valentine's Day.** The Millbrook Press, 1995.

Organizations and Online Sites

Festivals.com
RSL Interactive
1101 Alaskan Way
Pier 55, Suite 300
Seattle, WA 98101
http://www.festivals.com/

Visit this site to find out about all types of festivals, holidays, and fairs around the world.

The Holiday Page
http://www.wilstar.com/holidays

Find out about your favorite celebrations at this site, which is devoted to the holidays throughout the year.

Activity Idea Page
http://www.123child.com

This site suggests arts and crafts, games, and songs to use during many holidays and other activities during the year.

Important Words

ancient very, very old or from very early in history

commercial something that is made by machine in large numbers to be sold to many people

Cupid a young Roman god who made people fall in love by shooting them through the heart with invisible arrows

legend an old story that may be fact or fiction

pair to match or to put together

saint a good and holy person, or one who died for his or her religious beliefs

symbol something that stands for something else

tradition a custom, an idea, or a belief that is passed on through history

urn a jar or vase

Index

Meet the Author

Ever since Dana Meachen Rau can remember, she has loved to write. A graduate of Trinity College in Hartford, Connecticut, Dana works as a children's book editor and has authored many books for children, including biographies, nonfiction, early readers, and historical fiction. She has also won writing awards for her short stories.

When Dana is not writing, she is doing her favorite things—watching movies, eating chocolate, and drawing pictures—with her husband, Chris, and son, Charlie, in Farmington, Connecticut.